'How to . . .' A step-by-step guide to using:

Word XP

GW00697457

client ✓

Contents

✔ To access the PowerPoint Pop-Up Menu

The PowerPoint **Pop-Up menu** allows you to carry out a range of functions whilst in **Slide Show View**. This includes stopping the presentation and moving to the next and previous slide. This menu is only available when there are **no** annotations on the slide.

1. Press on the middle button of the **Slide Show toolbar.**

2. Choose **PowerPoint Commands** and then **Show PowerPoint Menu.**

   The PowerPoint Pop-Up Menu will appear.

3. Press the **SMART Board** to make the PowerPoint Pop-Up Menu disappear.

✔ To black out the PowerPoint presentation

If you wish to divert attention away from your PowerPoint presentation you can temporarily black out the display. You can then resume the presentation when you are ready.

1. Press on the middle button of the **Slide Show toolbar.**

2. Choose **PowerPoint Commands** and then **Black/Unblack Screen.**

SMART
Technologies Inc.

Contents

client ✓

PowerPoint XP

✔ To print a PowerPoint slide

1. Open a **PowerPoint** file.

2. Press on **Slide Show** and then **View Show**.

3. Press on the middle button of the **Slide Show toolbar**.

4. Choose **PowerPoint Commands** and then **Print Slide.**

   Your annotations plus an image of the slide will be sent to your printer.

✔ To clear and restore PowerPoint annotations

Having added annotations to your PowerPoint presentation you may then wish to clear these. If you wish to you can then restore previously cleared annotations.

✔ To clear annotations

1. Press on the middle button of the **Slide Show toolbar**.

2. Choose **Clear Annotations.**

   All annotations on the current slide will be cleared.

✔ To restore annotations

1. Press on the middle button of the **Slide Show toolbar**.

2. Choose **Restore Annotations.**

   The last annotation(s) to be cleared from the slide will be restored.

✔ Saving, opening and closing your document

Saving your documents enables you to store and retrieve work that you have undertaken. This allows you to review, edit and re-use these documents in the future.

✔ To save your document

1. Click on **File** and then **Save As**.

2. Click in the **File name** box and enter the name of your document e.g. **test**.

3. Click on the **Save** button.

4. To save again click on the **Save** icon on the toolbar.

✔ To save your document on a floppy disk

1. Click on **File** and then **Save As**.

2. Next to the **Save in** box click on the down arrow and choose **3½ Floppy**.

3. Click in the **File name** box and enter the name of your document e.g. **test**.

4. Click on the **Save** button.

PowerPoint XP

✔ To advance the slide with a single press

1. Press the middle button of the **Slide Show toolbar**.

2. Press on **Settings** and then de-select **Double-press to Advance**.

✔ To save annotations into PowerPoint

1. Open a **PowerPoint** file.

2. Press on **Slide Show** and then **View Show**.

3. Pick up the **Pen Tray Stylus** and write on the slide.

4. Press the middle button of the **Slide Show toolbar**.

5. Choose **Save Annotations to PowerPoint**.

✔ To automatically save annotations into PowerPoint

1. Press the middle button of the **Slide Show toolbar**.

2. Choose **Settings** and then **Auto-Save Annotations on Slide Advance**.

'How to . . .' A step-by-step guide to using:

Word XP

✔ To open an existing document

1. Click on **File** and **Open**.

2. Click on the document you want to open and then click on **Open**.

✔ To close the document

Click on **File** and then **Close**.

✔ To exit from Word

Click on **File** and then **Exit.**

✔ Special keys

The following special keys on the keyboard are especially useful when you wish to move around and edit a document on-screen.

✔ To use Backspace and Delete

1. Type the following sentence:

    The sun is shining.

2. Press the **Backspace** key. This deletes the text to the left of the cursor.

3. Press the **Delete** key. This deletes the text to the right of the cursor.

✔ To use PowerPoint on a SMART Board

Using **PowerPoint** with a **SMART Board** allows you to write over the top of your presentation, to save the slide with your annotations and to easily navigate forward and backward through a presentation.

✔ To move forward and backward using the Slide Show toolbar

1. Open your **PowerPoint** presentation.

2. Press on **Slide Show** and then **View Show**.

3. Use the two arrow buttons within the **Slide Show toolbar** to move forward and backward.

✔ To move forward using a double-press (right-orientated)

Double press anywhere on the board to move forward one slide.

This double press must be **right-oriented** i.e. press once and then again to the right of the first press.

✔ To move backward using a double-press (left-orientated)

Double press anywhere on the board to move back one slide.

This double press must be **left-oriented** i.e. press once and then again to the left of the first press.

SMART
Technologies Inc.

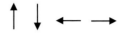

✔ To use the cursor movement keys ↑ ↓ ← →

1.   You can use the cursor movement keys to move your cursor to a new position within your sentence.

✔ To use Home and End

1.   Click at the beginning of your sentence and press **End**. This will move the cursor to the end of the line.

2.   Now press **Home**. This will move the cursor to the beginning of the line.

✔ To use Page up and page down

1.   Press the Page Up or PgUp key to move up one screen.

2.   Press the Page Down or PgDn key to move down one screen.

✔ To use Insert

1.   Place your cursor where you want to insert your text and press the **Insert** key once.

     Now as you type you will <u>type over</u> the existing text.

2.   Press the **Insert** key again to <u>insert</u> text within the existing text.

     NB: When you are in **type over** mode an **OVR** indicator will appear at the bottom of your screen.

| Page 1 | Sec 1 | 1/1 | At 25mm | Ln 1 | Col 8 | REC | TRK | EXT | OVR |

✔ To record narration

Rather than 'speaking to' your presentation you may prefer to record narration to accompany the slides presented. This may be particularly useful where you may not actually be present when the presentation is shown to a particular audience.

1.   Plug in your microphone.

2.   Click on **Slide Show** and then **Record Narration**.

3.   Click on **OK**.

4.   Your presentation will now be launched. As you click through the presentation, give your narration out loud.

5.   At the end of your presentation you will be asked **Do you want to save the slide timings also?** Click on **Yes**.

6.   Now when you view your presentation the narration will automatically be delivered.

✔ Formatting text

Formatting the text involves changing its appearance and includes aligning, underlining, emboldening, italicising and changing the font style, size and colour.   Such formatting can be used to enhance the appearance of your document.

If the formatting toolbar is not open click on **View**, **Toolbars** and then **Formatting**.

✔ To align text

Clicking on the alignment buttons changes the alignment of the current paragraph. You can align text on the **left**, in the **centre**, on the **right** or **justify** it (like newspapers where the text is straight on both sides).

✔ To underline text

1. Click on the **Underline** button on the toolbar and then type in your text.

2. Click on the **Underline** button again to turn underlining off.

✔ To embolden text

1. To embolden text click on the **Bold** Button on the toolbar.

2. Type in the text you want to embolden.

3. Click on the **Bold** button again to turn bold off.

✔ To run your presentation continuously

Often when making a presentation to an audience you will wish to 'speak to' the items presented on-screen and so will move from the beginning to the end of your presentation and no more. However, there may be occasions when you want to set up your presentation to run continuously e.g. during an exhibition.

1. Ensure that all of your slide transitions and animations are set to run automatically.

2. Click on **Slide Show** and then **Set Up Show**.

3. Select **Loop continuously until 'Esc'**.

4. Click on **OK**.

To italicise text

1. To italicise text click on the **Italic** Button on the toolbar.

2. Type in the text you want to italicise.

3. Click on the **Italic** button again to turn italics off.

To change the font style

1. Click on the arrow next to **Times New Roman**.

2. Choose a Font style from the list e.g. **Arial**.

To change the font size

1. Click on the arrow next to **12**.

2. Choose a Font size from the list e.g. **14**.

To change the font colour

1. Click on the arrow next to **Font colour**.

2. Choose a colour from the selection shown.

To change (format) the text after it has been typed

1. Highlight the piece of text you want to change.

2. Click on the appropriate button on the toolbar e.g. **Bold**.

To change the colour scheme

This facility enables you to choose one of a selection of colour schemes or to create one of your own. In this way you can choose the colour of the background and text and apply this to one or all of your slides.

1. Click on **Format** and then **Slide Design**.

2. Select **Colour Schemes** from the **Task Pane**.

3. Place your cursor over the colour scheme of your choice and click on the drop-down arrow.

4. Select **Apply to Selected Slides** to apply the colour scheme to this slide or **Apply to All** to apply this colour scheme to all the slides within your presentation.

To customise the colour scheme

1. Click on **Format** and then **Slide Design**.

2. Select **Colour Schemes** from the **Task Pane**.

3. Select **Edit Colour Schemes** from the bottom of the **Task Pane**.

4. Select from the list the scheme colour you wish to change e.g. **Background**.

5. Click on **Change Colour**.

6. Click on the colour of your choice and then **OK**.

7. Click on **Apply** to apply this colour scheme to all the slides within your presentation.

✔ To add Clip Art

The addition of Clip Art to your documents can enhance its appearance and usefully illustrate your text. Graphics can be imported from the Clip Art gallery and if you have internet access are also available on-line.

1. Click on **Insert**.

2. Click on **Picture**.

3. Click on **Clip Art**.

4. Click in **Search for** box displayed in the **Task Pane** and type the name of the image you require.

5. Click **Go**.

6. Click on the picture you wish to **Insert** into the document.

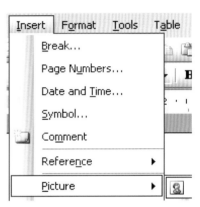

✔ To change the size

1. Click on your picture.

2. Holding down the left mouse button drag the handles in or out to make the picture larger or smaller.

✔ To change the position

1. Double click on the picture.

2. Select the **Layout** tab and click on **Square**.

3. Click on **OK**.

4. Point to the middle of the picture and, holding the left mouse button down, drag the picture to its new position.

To use Slide Transitions

Slide Transition refers to the way in which one slide moves into the next. Slides can simply appear or you can add effects such as **Box In** or **Wipe Up** to add interest to your presentation.

1. Create two or more slides of your presentation.

2. Click on **Slide Show** and then **Slide Transition**.

3. Choose a transition from the list in the **Task Pane** e.g. **Cover Left**.

4. Click on the down arrow next to **Speed** then select **Slow, Medium** or **Fast**.

5. Click on the down arrow next to **Sound** and then choose a sound e.g. **Camera**.

6. Click on **Apply to All Slides** to apply this to all of the slides within your presentation.

✔ To add WordArt

WordArt can be used to enhance the appearance of your document and is particularly useful when you are creating documents such as fliers and posters which need to be eye-catching.

1. Click on **Insert** and then **Picture.**

2. Click on **Word Art** and select the style you would like to use.

3. Click on **OK**.

4. Choose the font style and size you want to use.

5. Type in your text and click on **OK**.

✔ To use the drawing tools

The drawing toolbar enables you to add Clip Art, WordArt, AutoShapes, lines and arrows to your documents. These can be useful in adding interest to your work and for creating diagrams and illustrations to your work.

PowerPoint

 To change the order of your animation

Once you have animated your text or graphics you may wish to change the order in which they appear in your presentation. For example, you may wish your text to appear before your illustrations.

1. Click on **Slide Show** and **Custom Animation**.

2. In the **Task Pane** select an item from the list.

3. Use the **Re-Order** buttons to move each item into its correct order of appearance.

 Re-Order

✔ To open the Drawing toolbar (if not open)

1. Click on **View** and then **Toolbars**.

2. Select **Drawing**. The drawing toolbar will now appear at the bottom of the screen.

✔ To use the Drawing Canvas

N.B Once any mode of drawing is selected, the Drawing Canvas will automatically open. Clicking anywhere outside the **Drawing Canvas** will remove this option.

Using the **Drawing Canvas** will allow you to draw multiple shapes which can be moved about as a collective group.

✔ To move shapes as a group

1. Select and draw the shapes you wish to move on the **Drawing Canvas.**

2. Double click inside the **Drawing Canvas**.

3. Select the **Layout** Tab and click on **Square**.

4. Click on **OK**.

5. Point to edge of the **Drawing Canvas** and, holding the left mouse button down, drag the Canvas to its new position.

6. Click on the small solid black lines in the inside corner of the **Drawing Canvas** and, keeping the mouse button held down, drag the mouse to increase or decrease the size of the **Drawing Canvas** area.

 client ✔

Drawing tools

8

✔ Editing your presentation

Within **Slide Sorter View** you can copy, delete or re-order your slides. This will enable you to quickly and easily customize your presentation to suit a particular audience.

✔ To delete slides

1. Click on **View** and then **Slide Sorter View** or click on the icon.

2. Click on the slide you wish to delete and press **Delete** on your keyboard.

✔ To copy slides

1. Click on **View** and then **Slide Sorter View** or click on the icon.

2. Click on the slide you wish to copy.

3. Click on **Edit** and then **Copy**.

4. Click where you wish your new slide (the copy) to be placed e.g. next to this one.

5. Click on **Edit** and then **Paste**.

✔ To change the order of your slides

1. Click on **View** and then **Slide Sorter View** or click on the icon.

2. Point to the slide you wish to move, hold down your left mouse button and drag the slide into its new position.

To draw lines, arrows, rectangles or ovals

1. Click on the **Line**, **Arrow**, **Rectangle** or **Oval** icon.

2. Click where you want to start drawing and keeping the mouse button held down drag the mouse to increase / decrease the size of the line or shape.

3. Release the mouse button and the line or shape will appear.

4. To change the style of an arrow click on the **Arrow Style** icon and click on the arrow of your choice.

5. To change the thickness or line style of your line or shape click on the **Line Style** or **Dash Style** icon and click on the style of your choice.

6. To change the colour of your line or shape click on the down arrow next to the **Line Colour** icon and select the colour of your choice.

✔ To use the 'Master Slide'

The **Master Slide** allows you to create elements common to all slides. This can include elements such as the background and graphics. All of the features added to the **Master Slide** will appear on every slide in your presentation.

1. Click on **View** and then **Master**.

2. Click on **Slide Master**.

3. Select the title box and change the font style and size as appropriate.

4. Select the text box and change the font style and size as appropriate.

5. Add a background by clicking on **Format**, **Background**, clicking on the down arrow and selecting a colour or **Fill Effect** of your choice, clicking on **OK** and then **Apply**.

6. Add clip art by clicking on **Insert**, **Picture**, **Clip Art**, selecting a picture and clicking on **Insert**.

7. Click on **Close Master View** to return to your presentation.

✔ To add AutoShapes

AutoShapes ▾

1. Click on the **AutoShapes** button.

2. Click on the type of shape you would like e.g. **Basic Shapes.**

3. Click on a shape of your choice.

4. Hold down the left mouse button and drag the mouse to increase or decrease the size of the shape.

✔ To rotate an AutoShape

1. Click on the shape you wish to rotate.

2. Click on the green spot that appears on the top of your shape.

3. Hold down your left mouse button whilst you drag the shape to rotate it.

✔ To add shadow to an AutoShape

1. Click on the shape you wish to add shadow to.

2. Click on the **Shadow Style** icon.

✔ To change a 2D AutoShape into a 3D shape

1. Click on the shape to which you wish to change to 3D.

2. Click on the **3-D Style** icon.

PowerPoint XP

✔To include movies in your presentation

PowerPoint offers you the facility to incorporate moving images within your presentation. These can be quickly and easily inserted from the Clip Organizer or from file if you have your own movie clips saved there.

1. Load PowerPoint.

2. Select an **AutoLayout** of your choice and click on **OK**.

3. Click on **Insert** and then **Movies and Sounds**.

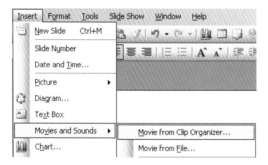

4. Click on **Movie from Clip Organizer**.

5. Click on the movie clip you wish to **Insert** into your presentation.

6. Move and / or re-size the movie as appropriate.

7. To view your movie click on **Slide Show** and then **View Show**.

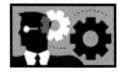

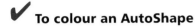
✔ To colour an AutoShape

1. Click on the **AutoShape**.

2. Click on the **Fill Colour** icon on the drawing tool bar.

3. To select a different colour click on the down arrow next to the **Fill Colour** icon and click on the colour of your choice.

✔ To add a Page Border

Adding page borders to your documents can make them more appealing and is useful when designing documents such as advertisements and certificates.

1. Click on **Format**.

2. Click on **Borders and Shading**.

3. Click on the **Page Border** tab.

4. Click on the **Art** down arrow.

5. Select a border and click on **OK**.

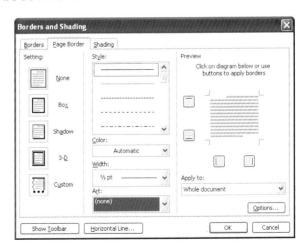

✔ To insert a sound clip

The addition of sound clips to your presentation enables you to record and attach relevant sounds (e.g. narration) to your work. The reader can then access this sound clip by clicking on the icon displayed.

Make sure you have a microphone plugged in first.

1. Click on **Insert**.

2. Click on **Object**.

3. Scroll down to **Wave Sound**.

4. Click **OK**. This will launch your sound recorder which works in exactly the same way as a tape recorder.

5. Press record (red circle) and speak into the microphone.

6. Press stop (black square).

7. This symbol should appear on your slide.

8. You can hear what you have recorded by double clicking on the symbol.

✔ To insert existing sound clips

1. Click on **Insert** and then click on **Object**.

2. Scroll down to **Wave Sound** and then select **Create from file**.

3. Click on **Browse** to locate your file and select it.

To change the page orientation

The documents you produce can be viewed and printed either in **Portrait** or **Landscape** orientation according to your needs. Documents such as letters are likely to be presented in Portrait, whereas something like a timetable may use Landscape.

1. Click on **File** and **Page Setup**.

2. Click on **Landscape**.

3. Click on **OK**.

To use print preview

Print preview enables you to view your document before you send it to print. In this way you can easily check the layout of your document and amend it as needed.

1. Click on **File** and then **Print Preview**.

2. Click on **Close** to return to your work.

✔ To add Action Buttons

Normally PowerPoint will progress through its slides in the order they are stored but it is possible to add Action Buttons which will, when clicked, take the reader to other slides.

1. Click on **Slide Show** and then **Action Buttons**.

2. Click on the Action Button of your choice.

3. Click on your slide and drag the button to the right size.

4. A dialog box will pop up. If this does not happen, point to the button and click your right mouse button and select **Action Settings**.

5. Choose the slide you want to link to from the list and click on **OK**.

✔ Cut, copy, paste

Cut, **Copy** and **Paste** allow you to quickly and easily edit and redraft your text. In this way you can change the order of sentences or paragraphs and remove unwanted text, or even copy useful items which can then be pasted elsewhere in this or any other document.

✔ To move a block of text

1. Highlight the section to be moved by **dragging** with the mouse from the start to the end.

2. Click on **Cut** on the toolbar.

3. Move the cursor to the new position.

4. Click on **Paste** on the toolbar.

✔ To copy a block of text

1. Highlight the section to be copied by **dragging** with the mouse from the start to the end.

2. Click on **Copy** on the toolbar.

3. Move the cursor to the new position.

4. Click on **Paste** on the toolbar.

✔ To use the View menu

The View menu allows you to view your work on-screen in a variety of ways. You may prefer to work on your presentation in **Slide View** but check the order of slides in **Slide Sorter View**.

1. Click on **View** and then **Normal View** or click on the icon.

2. Click on **View** and then **Slide Sorter View** or click on the icon.

3. Click on **View** and then **Notes Page**.

4. Click on **View** and then **Slide Show** or click on the icon.

View	Insert	Format	Tools
📄 Normal			
⊞ Slide Sorter			
🖥 Slide Show		F5

✔ To check spelling

Word offers the useful feature of checking your spelling within a document. In this way you can check for errors before you print your work.

1. Click on the **Spelling and Grammar** button on the toolbar.

2. Click on the correct spelling in the **Suggestions box** and click on **Change** to replace the word.

   OR

   Click on **Ignore** to leave it as it is.

3. If the dictionary does not list the appropriate answer, click in the **Not in dictionary** box and type in the correct spelling. Then click on **Change**.

4. Click on **Cancel** to finish spell checking.

✔ To check the word count

Checking how many words you have written within your document can be useful where you have been set a particular word count for a piece of work, e.g. if you are writing a synopsis of a larger document.

1. Click on **Tools** and then **Word Count**. Your word count will then be displayed.

2. Click on **Close** to return to your work.

To add graphics saved on file to your presentation

In addition to using Clip Art from the Clip Organizer you may wish to add to your presentation graphics you have previously saved. These can include those you have scanned and / or taken with a digital camera.

1. Click on **Insert**.

2. Click on **Picture**.

3. Click on **From File**.

4. Select the folder in which you have saved the graphic.

5. Click on the graphic file that you wish to use.

6. Click on **Insert**.

To copy graphics from another document

Documents you have previously created may contain graphics you wish to re-use. These too can be copied and pasted into another document.

1. Point to the graphic (picture) you wish to copy.

2. Right click the mouse and click on **Copy**.

3. Open the document you wish to paste the graphic into.

4. Click on **Edit** and then **Paste**.

Word XP

✔ To zoom in and out

Zooming in and out can be useful when you are creating documents where the layout is important. Zooming in allows you to easily read and edit the text on-screen but only allows you to see part of the document at a time. Zooming out enables you to check the overall appearance of the document.

1. Click on the **Zoom** down arrow and choose e.g. **50%**. This will reduce the size of your page.

2. Click on the **Zoom** down arrow and choose **Page Width** to return your page to its normal size.

✔ To add page numbers

Adding page numbers can be useful where you have created a large document. It allows the reader to easily order the loose pages and enables the writer to refer readers to particular pages in the document.

1. Click on **Insert** on the toolbar and then **Page Numbers.**

2. Click on the down arrow and select the **Position** of the page number e.g. **Bottom of page.**

3. Click on the down arrow and select the **Alignment** of the page number e.g. **Right**.

4. Click on **OK.**

To add borders

1. Right click on the **Table** and then select **Borders and Fill**.

2. Click on the **Borders** tab.

3. Click on the down arrows to choose a **Line Style**, **Colour** and **Width**.

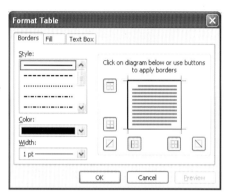

4. Click on the relevant buttons on the diagram to apply the borders to your table.

5. Click on **OK**.

To colour the cells

1. Click in the cell or highlight the row / column you wish to colour.

2. Click on **Table** and then **Borders and Fill**.

3. Click on the **Fill** tab.

4. Click on the down arrows to choose a **Colour**.

5. Click on **OK**.

✔ To insert a page break

Inserting a page break enables you to force a break at a point in the text convenient to you. For example, if a page naturally breaks in the middle of a paragraph you may wish to insert a page break before the start of this paragraph in order to improve the appearance of your document.

1. Place the cursor at the point in your document where you wish to create a page break.

2. Click on **Insert** and then **Break**.

3. Select the **Page break** option and then click on **OK**.

✔ To remove paragraph codes

Paragraph codes allow you to see where you have entered returns (i.e. pressed **Enter** or **Return** on your keyboard) and created page breaks. By viewing and deleting these you can easily join two paragraphs together or remove page breaks should you wish to.

1. Click on the **Show / Hide** button on the standard toolbar. The screen will now change to show the codes in the text.

   This shows you where you have pressed **Enter** or inserted a **Page break**.

2. If you want to join two paragraphs together place the cursor next to the code and press the **Delete** key.

3. Click on the **Show / Hide** button again to return to your normal screen.

✔ To create a table

Tables allow you to organise information clearly within columns and rows. They can be created for a wide variety of purposes e.g. to present data or timetable.

1. Click on **Insert** and then **Table**.

2. Choose the number of columns and rows you would like.

3. Click on **OK**.

4. Drag the table into the correct position on your slide.

✔ To add columns

1. Click on **Table** and then **Insert Columns to the Left** or **Insert Columns to the Right**.

2. Then re-size the table by dragging the re-sizing handles around its edge.

✔ To add rows

1. Click on **Table** and then **Insert Rows Above** or **Insert Rows Below**.

2. Then re-size the table by dragging the re-sizing handles around its edge.

✔ To use line numbering

Line numbering can be useful if you wish to number paragraphs or sentences within your text. This can help you and the reader locate and refer to items within your document.

1. Type in the following list:

   Literacy
   Numeracy
   Science
   ICT

2. Highlight the four topics by **dragging** the pointer across them.

3. Click on the **Numbering** button on the formatting toolbar.

✔ To use bullets

Adding bullet points can be useful if you are creating a list of items or sentences within a document. This can help you present your information more clearly.

1. Type in the following list:
   Red
   Blue
   Green
   Yellow

2. Highlight the four topics by **dragging** the pointer across them.

3. Click on the **Bullets** button on the formatting toolbar.

client ✔

6. Click in each box and add your own text, e.g. the name and position of each individual in the organisation.

7. To add further boxes to the chart, click on the box to which you wish to attach a new box. Then click on **Insert Shape** on the **Organization Chart toolbar** and select the appropriate item e.g. **Subordinate**.

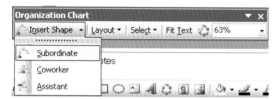

Repeat this process until you have added all the necessary items to the chart.

8. To remove a box from the chart, select the box and then press delete on your keyboard.

9. Click the cross on the **Organization Chart toolbar** to close it and return to your presentation.

✔ To animate text

Text animation allows you to add sparkle and other effects to text. Invitations or greetings cards which are opened and viewed by readers on-screen are examples of documents where the use of text animation might be appropriate.

1.   Enter your text.

2.   Highlight the text you wish to animate.

3.   Click on **Format** and then **Font**.

4.   Click on the **Text Effects** or **Animation** tab.

5.   Click on an animation from the list e.g. **Sparkle Text**.

6.   Click on **OK**.

✔ To add Text Boxes to your document

Text boxes are useful if you wish to place text in a particular place e.g. next to a picture. Please see page 8 for use of the **Drawing Canvas**.

1.   Click on **Insert** and then **Text Box**. A symbol similar to a plus sign will appear.

2.   Hold down the left mouse button and drag the mouse to increase / decrease the size of the box.

3.   Type your text in the Text Box.

✔ To include organisational charts in a presentation

The inclusion of organisational charts within your presentation can be useful where you wish to give an indication of the hierarchical structure of an organisation, family trees or classification keys.

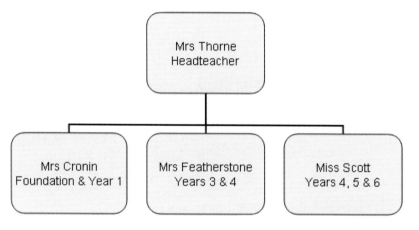

1. Click on **Insert** and then **New Slide**.

2. Click on a **Slide Layout** from the **Content Layout** or **Text and Content Layout** area of the **Task Pane**.

3. Click on the **Insert Diagram** or **Organization Chart** icon on the slide.

4. A **Diagram Gallery** will appear.

5. Select the **Organization Chart** and click **OK**.

continued...

✔ To colour a Text Box

1. Click on the Text Box.

2. Click on the **Fill Colour** icon on the drawing tool bar.

3. To select a different colour click on the down arrow next to the **Fill Colour** icon and click on the colour of your choice.

✔ To use Find and Replace

Find and Replace can be useful where you wish to edit one or more key words within a document without having to locate and amend them on an individual basis. For example, if you wished to replace all references to 'Susan' within a report, you could substitute this word wherever it occurs within a document. In this way you can easily amend documents you have previously created.

1. Highlight the text you want to use (or click on **Edit** and then **Select All** if you want to use the whole text).

2. Click on **Edit** and then **Replace**.

3. In the **Find what** box type in the word you want to find e.g. **IT**.

4. In the **Replace with** box type in the letter or symbol you want to replace it with e.g. **ICT**.

5. Click on **Replace All**.

✔ **To include graphs and charts in a presentation**

Graphs and charts can be usefully incorporated within a presentation particularly where you wish to present data to your audience. Such a visual representation can be an effective means of presenting data, allowing your audience to quickly and easily identify the patterns and trends.

1. Click on **Insert** and then **New Slide**.

2. Click on a **Slide Layout** from the **Content Layout** or **Text and Content Layout** area of the **Task Pane**.

3. Click on the **Insert Chart** icon on the slide.

4. A datasheet will now appear. Replace the data it contains with your own. For example:

		A	B	C	D	E
		Bill	Sharma	Tracy	Ollie	
1	1st attempt	10	12	9	4	
2	2nd attempt	12	11	5	5	
3	3rd attempt	12	9	8	5	

Presentation1 - Datasheet

5. Click on the cross to close this window and your chart will have been added to your presentation.

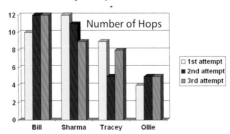

✔ To create a table

Tables allow you to organise information within columns and rows, and to organise your information clearly. They can be created for a wide variety of purposes e.g. to present data, make plans or create timetables.

1. Click on **Table** on the toolbar.

2. Click on **Insert** then click on **Table**.

3. Type in the number of rows and columns and click on **OK**.

✔ To move between each cell of your table

Press the tab key, or point and click with the mouse.

✔ To merge cells together

1. Highlight the relevant parts of your table.

2. Click on **Table** and **Merge Cells**.

✔ To change the text direction

1. Highlight the relevant row(s) / column(s).

2. Click on **Format** and then **Text Direction**.

3. Click on the text orientation of your choice.

4. Click on **OK**.

✔ To apply a Design Template

Design Templates enable you to apply one of a range of interesting background designs to all of the slides within your presentation.

1. Click on **Format**.

2. Click on **Slide Design**.

3. Click on the picture of the template design of your choice from the **Task Pane**.

✔ **To centre the text vertically within a cell**

1. Highlight the relevant row(s).

2. Click on **Format**.

3. Click on **Paragraph**.

4. In the paragraph box, under the section headed **Spacing**, change **Before** and **After** boxes from 0pt to 6pt.

5. Click on **OK**.

✔ **To remove the borders**

1. Highlight the table and click on the Borders button on the formatting toolbar and click the relevant borders off.

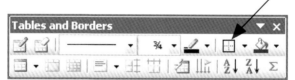

✔ **To change the border around the cells**

1. Highlight the cell(s) that you wish to have borders.

2. Click on **Format** and **Borders and Shading**.

3. Click on the **Borders** tab and select the border you require.

4. Click on **OK**.

✔ How to print your presentation

It is often useful to print out a copy of your presentation as notes for yourself or for your audience. Usefully in PowerPoint you can choose to print your presentation using a variety of formats.

1. Click on **File** and then **Print**.

2. Choose **All**, **Current slide** or **Selection.**.

3. If you would like to print a selection of slides enter the slide numbers e.g. **1-3** in the box next to **Slides.**

4. Choose the number of copies.

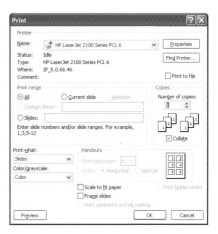

5. Click on the down arrow next to **Print what** and choose either

   - **Slides** (one slide per page)
   - **Handouts** (two or more slides per page with room to write notes)
   - **Notes Pages** (one slide plus notes per page)
   - **Outline View** (an outline of your presentation)

6. If you have chosen **Handouts** click on the down arrow next to **Slides per page** to choose a number between 2 & 9.

7. Click on **OK**.

To change the height and width of a cell

1. Point to the dividing line between two columns or rows. You will see a two-headed arrow appear.

2. Hold your left mouse button down and drag the line to make the column or row wider.

 To insert a column

1. Click in the column where you wish to add another column.

2. Click on **Table** and then **Insert**.

3. Click on **Column to the Right** or **Column to the left**.

 To insert a row

1. Click in the row where you wish to add another row.

2. Click on **Table** and then **Insert**.

3. Click on **Rows Above** or **Rows Below**.

 To make all your columns or rows the same width

1. Highlight your table.

2. Click on **Tables** and then **Autofit**.

3. Click on **Distribute Columns Evenly** or **Distribute Rows Evenly**.

✔ To create sound effects

Having first animated your text or graphics you can also choose to add sound effects to accompany the effects you have selected. There is a range of sound effects you can choose from including **Chime**, **Whoosh** and **Drum Roll**.

1. Click on **Slide Show** and **Custom Animation**.

2. In the **Task Pane**, select the custom animation you want to add sound to.

3. Click on the drop-down arrow and select **Effect Options**.

4. Click on the drop-down arrow next to the sound box and select the sound of your choice e.g. **Applause** and click on **OK**.

✔ To run your slide show

Whilst you may choose to use PowerPoint to create a variety of documents, it is particularly useful as a presentational tool. By running or viewing your presentation you can share this with an audience. This is especially effective if you are able to use a data projector and large screen.

1. Click on **Slide Show** and **View Show**.

2. Click your mouse to animate text or Clip Art.

✔ To add shading

1. Highlight the part of your table that you wish to add shading to.

2. Click on **Format** and then **Borders and Shading**.

3. Click on the **Shading** tab.

4. Click on the shade or colour of your choice.

5. Click on **OK**.

✔ To sort data in your table

Name	Age
Hazel	5
Paul	15
Gemma	8
James	10
Shirley	12

1. Click in your table.

2. Click on **Table** and then **Sort**.

3. Under **Sort by** choose the column you want to sort e.g. **Name**.

4. Click on **OK**.

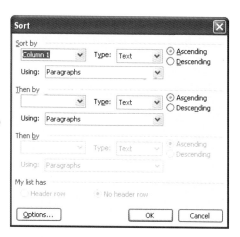

✔ To animate text or Clip Art

1. Click on the Text Box or Clip Art you want to animate.

2. Click on **Slide Show** and **Custom Animation**.

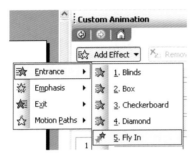

3. Click on **Add Effect** from the **Task Pane** and select an animation of your choice from one of the four options e.g. **Entrance**, **Fly in**.

The direction, speed and timing of animation can be altered by using the drop-down arrows in the **Task Pane** next to **Start**, **Direction** and **Speed**.

4. Click on the **Order & Timing** tab.

5. Under **Start animation** select **On mouse click** or **Automatically.**

6. If you have chosen **Automatically** choose the number of seconds delay before you wish the item to appear e.g. **00:05**.

7. Click on **OK**.

✔ To create columns

Creating columns within your document is useful if you are creating a newsletter or a flier. You can choose to have one, two or three columns depending on the effect you are trying to create.

1. Click on **Format** and then **Columns**.

2. Choose e.g. **Two** and then click on **OK**.

3. As you type your text will now be organised into two columns.

✔ To add graphics saved on file

In addition to using Clip Art from the Clip Organizer you may wish to add to your document graphics you have previously saved. These can include those you have scanned and / or taken with a digital camera.

1. Click on **Insert**.

2. Click on **Picture**.

3. Click on **From File**.

4. Select the folder in which you have saved the graphic.

5. Click on the graphic file that you wish to use.

6. Click on **Insert**.

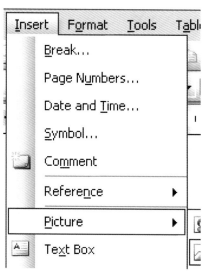

✔ To insert a new slide

A presentation created in PowerPoint can be made up of one or many slides. When you insert a new slide you can select a new AutoLayout and so create a varied and interesting presentation.

1. Click on **Insert** and then **New Slide**.

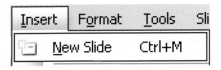

2. Click on the **Slide Layout** of your choice in the **Task Pane**.

3. Click on **OK**.

✔ To copy text from another document

There may often be occasions when you wish to copy and paste text from one document to another. You can then edit and re-format the text to suit your needs.

1. Highlight the text you wish to copy by holding down the left mouse button and dragging over the text e.g. from left to right.

2. Click on **Edit** and then **Copy**.

3. Open the document you wish to paste the text into.

    NB: If you are switching from one application to another (e.g. PowerPoint to Word) hold down the **Alt** key and press the **Tab** key. Continue to hold down **Alt** and press the **Tab** key until you select the application you want to switch to.

4. Click on **Edit** and then **Paste**.

✔ To copy graphics from another document

Documents you have previously created may contain graphics you wish to re-use. These too can be copied and pasted into another document.

1. Point to the graphic (picture) you wish to copy.

2. Right click the mouse and click on **Copy**.

3. Open the document you wish to paste the graphic into.

4. Click on **Edit** and then **Paste**.

PowerPoint XP

 To change a 2D AutoShape into a 3D shape

1. Click on the shape you wish to change to 3D.

2. Click on the **3-D Style** icon.

 To colour an Autoshape

1. Click on the **AutoShape**.

2. Click on the **Fill Colour** icon on the drawing tool bar.

3. To select a different colour click on the down arrow next to the **Fill Colour** icon and click on the colour of your choice.

Word XP

✔ To use the Office Clipboard

The Office Clipboard allows you to copy and hold up to 24 items which can then be pasted into your document wherever and whenever you choose. This can be useful if you are using a set of key words or phrases e.g. when writing reports.

1. Click on **Edit** and then **Office Clipboard**.

2. To add items to the clipboard select the text you wish to add, then click on the **Copy** icon.

3. To paste an item from your clipboard click on the relevant item on the clipboard.

5. To clear the clipboard click on the **Clear All** icon.

✔ Headers and footers

Headers and Footers allow you to add the same information to the top or bottom of every page in your document. For example, you may wish to add your name and the date your document was created to the Footer.

✔ To add AutoShapes

AutoShapes ▼

1. Click on the **AutoShapes** button.

2. Click on the type of shape you would like e.g. **Basic Shapes.**

3. Click on a shape of your choice.

4. Hold down the left mouse button and drag the mouse to increase or decrease the size of the shape.

✔ To rotate an AutoShape

1. Click on the shape you wish to rotate.

2. Click on the green spot that appears on the top of your shape.

3. Hold down your left mouse button whilst you drag the shape to rotate it.

✔ To add shadow to an AutoShape

1. Click on the shape you wish to add shadow to.

2. Click on the **Shadow Style** icon.

 To create a header

1. Click on **View** and then **Header and Footer**.

2. Type in your header e.g. **Sarah Peach**.

3. Click on **Close** to return to your document.

 To create a footer

1. Click on **View** and then **Header and Footer**.

2. Click on the **Switch Between Header and Footer** button within the Header window.

3. Type in your footer e.g. **Willensdale Primary School**.

4. Click on **Close** to return to your document.

 To add footnotes

Footnotes allow you to add comments to particular items within your text. For example, if you use an abbreviation e.g. ICT within your document you may wish to add a Footnote which explains the term to readers who are unfamiliar with it.

1. Place the cursor just after a key word in your work e.g. ICT.

2. Click on **Insert, Reference, Footnote** and then click on **Insert**.

3. Type in your footnote e.g. **Information and Communications Technology**.

✔ To use the drawing tools

The drawing toolbar enables you to add Clip Art, WordArt, AutoShapes, lines and arrows to your presentation. These can be useful in adding interest and for creating diagrams and illustrations.

✔ To open the Drawing toolbar (if not open)

1. Click on **View** and then **Toolbars**.

2. Select **Drawing**. The drawing toolbar will now appear at the bottom of the screen.

✔ To draw lines, arrows, rectangles or ovals

1. Click on the **Line**, **Arrow**, **Rectangle** or **Oval** icon.

2. Click where you want to start drawing and keeping the mouse button held down drag the mouse to increase or decrease the size of the line or shape.

3. Release the mouse button and the line or shape will appear.

4. To change the style of an arrow click on the **Arrow Style** icon and click on the arrow of your choice.

5. To change the thickness or line style of your line or shape click on the **Line Style** or **Dash Style** icon and click on the style of your choice.

6. To change the colour of your line or shape click on the down arrow next to the **Line Colour** icon and select the colour of your choice.

✔ To use the View menu

The View menu allows you to view your work on-screen in a variety of ways. You may prefer to work on your document in **Normal View** but look at your document in **Print Layout** before you send it to print so that you can check how it appears on the page.

To change the way your page appears on the screen:

1. Click on **View** and click on each of the following:

   • Normal Layout
   • Web Layout
   • Print Layout
   • Reading Layout

2. Click on View and then **Print Layout** to return to your normal view.

✔ To create Drop-Down lists in Word

Drop-Down lists can be useful where you are creating questionnaires or quizzes for use on-screen. By clicking on the Drop-Down list, users can select an answer from the list shown rather than having to type in their own.

1. Place your cursor where you want your list to appear.

2. Click on **View,** then click on **Toolbars** and then click **Forms**.

   A **Forms** toolbar will appear.

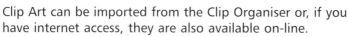

✔ To add Clip Art

Clip Art can be imported from the Clip Organiser or, if you have internet access, they are also available on-line.

1. Click on **Insert**.
2. Click on **Picture**.
3. Click on **Clip Art**.
4. Click in the **Search for** box displayed in the **Task Pane** and type the name of the image you require.
5. Click **Go**.
6. Click on the picture you wish to use to **Insert** into the presentation.

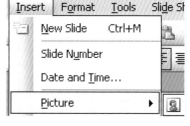

✔ To change the size

1. Click on your picture.
2. Holding down the left mouse button drag the handles in or out to make the picture larger or smaller.

✔ To change the position

1. Click on the picture.
2. Point to the middle of the picture and, holding the left mouse button down, drag the picture to its new position.

✔ To rotate the picture

1. Click on your picture.
2. Click on the green spot that appears at the top of your picture.
3. Hold down your left mouse button whilst you drag the picture to rotate it.

3. Click on the third button and a 'field' (grey area) will appear where your cursor is positioned.

4. Double click the field (grey area) and a window will appear.

5. Write your selection of 'answers' in the **drop-down item** list, clicking **Add** after each answer.

6. Then click **OK**.

7. Click the **Protect Form** to finish.

 To create a Pop-Up comment

Pop-Up comments can be created which appear when you point to a particular word or phrase within a document. These can be useful if you want to give readers access to more information. For example, you might want to provide a definition of key terms unfamiliar to your readers.

1. Highlight the text you wish to add your comment to.

2. Click on **Insert** and select **Comment**.

The following **Comment Balloon** will appear.

3. Type in your message.

4. Click back onto your document to continue typing.

5. Now when you point to the text your Pop-Up message will appear.

✔ To use line numbering

Line numbering can be useful if you wish to number paragraphs or sentences within your text. This can help you and the reader locate and refer to items within your presentation.

1. Type in the following list:
   Literacy
   Numeracy
   Science
   ICT

2. Highlight the four topics by dragging the pointer across them.

3. Click on the **Numbering** button on the toolbar.
   1. Literacy
   2. Numeracy
   3. Science
   4. ICT

✔ To use bullets

Adding bullet points can be useful if you are creating a list of items or sentences within a presentation. This can help you present your information more clearly.

1. Type in the following list:
   Red
   Blue
   Green
   Yellow

2. Highlight the four topics by dragging the pointer across them.

3. Click on the **Bullets** button on the toolbar.
   • Red
   • Blue
   • Green
   • Yellow

✔ To add Hyperlinks

Hyperlinks are used within documents to create links to other places within the same document, to other documents or to specific webpages.

In order to add hyperlinks to your documents you must first create bookmarks.

✔ To create Bookmarks within your text

1. Highlight the word or phrase you want to link from.

2. Click on **Insert** on the menu bar and then **Bookmark**.

3. Give the bookmark a name e.g. **one.**

4. Highlight the word or phrase you want to link this to.

5. Click on **Insert** on the menu bar and then **Bookmark**.

6. Give the bookmark a name e.g. **two.**

✔ To create Hyperlinks within your text

1. Highlight the word or phrase you want to link from.

2. Click on **Insert** on the menu bar and then **Hyperlink**.

3. Click on **Place in this document** (or click on the **Browse** button next to **Named location in file**).

4. Click on the name of the bookmark you want to link this to e.g. **two** and then click on **OK**.

✔ How to add Text Boxes

Text boxes are useful if you wish to place text in a particular place e.g. next to a picture.

1. Click on **Insert** and then **Text Box**.

    A symbol similar to a plus sign will appear.

2. Hold down the left mouse button and drag the mouse to increase or decrease the size of the box.

3. Type your text in the Text Box.

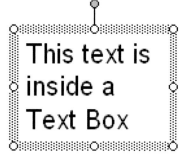

✔ To rotate Text Boxes

1. Click on the **Text Box**.

2. Click on the green spot that appears at the top of the **Text Box**.

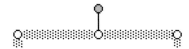

3. Hold down your left mouse button whilst you drag the **Text Box** to rotate it.

Word XP

✔ To insert a sound clip

The addition of sound clips to your documents enables you to record and attach relevant sounds (e.g. narration) to your work. The reader can then access this sound clip by clicking on the icon displayed.

Make sure you have a microphone plugged in first.

1.   Click on **Insert**.

2.   Click on **Object**.

3.   Scroll down to **Wave Sound**.

4.   Click **OK**. This will launch your sound recorder which works in exactly the same way as a tape recorder.

5.   Press record (red circle) and speak into the microphone.

6.   Press stop (black square).

7.   This symbol should appear.

8.   You can hear what you have recorded by double clicking on the symbol.

✔ To insert existing sound clips

1.   Click on **Insert** and then an **Object**.

2.   Scroll down to **Wave Sound** and then select **Create from file**.

3.   Click on **Browse** to locate your file and select it.

How to add a background

Adding a background to your slides can enhance their appearance. If you wish you can apply the same background to all slides within your presentation or apply a different background to each slide. Select from a wide range of colours, gradients, textures and patterns.

1. Click on **Format**.

2. Click on **Background**.

3. Click on down arrow.

4. Click on **Fill Effects**.

5. Select background from **Gradient, Pattern, Texture** or **Picture** tabs and click on **OK**.

Alternatively, create your own background by adding a picture from Clip Art and stretching it to fill the entire slide (see page 9).

✔ To create templates

Templates for frequently used documents such as letters and reports are useful in that they allow you to open a copy, amend as necessary and then save the document under a new name.

1. Having created your document click on **File** and **Save As**.

2. Enter a **File name** for your template.

3. Next to **Save as** type click on the down arrow and choose **Document Template**.

4. Click on **Save**.

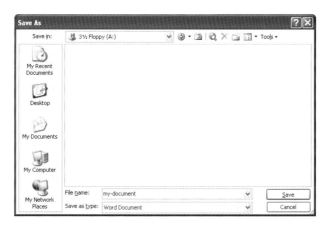

✔ To open a template

1. Click on **File** and then **Open**.

2. Click on the template you want to open, then click on **Open**.

✔ To change the font style

1. Click on the arrow next to **Arial**.

Arial ▾ 18 ▾

2. Choose a Font style from the list e.g. **Times New Roman**.

✔ To change the font size

1. Click on the arrow next to **18**.

Arial ▾ 18 ▾

2. Choose a Font size from the list e.g. **14**.

✔ To change the font colour

1. Click on the arrow next to **Font colour**.

2. Choose a colour from the selection shown.

✔ To change (format) the text after it has been typed

1. Highlight the piece of text you want to change.

2. Click on the appropriate button on the toolbar e.g. **Bold**.

B

✔ To create letters using Mail Merge

Mail Merge is the process of combining a standard letter and a list of items (such as names and addresses) to produce individualised copies of the letter.

1. Start by creating and saving your Data Source. Once this has been created you can use it again and again. To do, this type the names and address you wish to use either within a spreadsheet or within a table in Word. It should look something like this:

Name	Address1	Address2	Address3	Address4	PostCode
Heidi Barton	Canterbury Christ Church University College	North Holmes Road	Canterbury	Kent	CT1 1QU
Martin Williams	South East Essex College	Canarvon Road	Southend	Essex	SS0 1QU

2. Click on **Tools, Letters and Mailings** and then **Mail Merge**.

3. Follow the instructions as written in the **Task Pane**. You may click forward and back once you have started this process.

4. **Step 1** - Select the type of document you are working on e.g. **Letters**.

5. **Step 2** - Select the type of document you wish to use e.g. **Use the current document.**

✔ Formatting text

Formatting the text involves changing its appearance and includes aligning, underlining, emboldening, italicising and changing the font style, size and colour. Such formatting can be used to enhance the appearance of your presentation.

✔ To align text

Clicking on the alignment buttons changes the alignment of the current paragraph. You can align text on the **left**, in the **centre**, or on the **right**.

✔ To underline text

1. Click on the **Underline** button on the toolbar and then type in your text.

2. Click on the **Underline** button again to turn underlining off.

✔ To embolden text

1. To embolden text click on the **Bold** Button on the toolbar.

2. Type in the text you want to embolden.

3. Click on the **Bold** button again to turn bold off.

✔ To italicise text

1. To italicise text click on the **Italic** Button on the toolbar.

2. Type in the text you want to italicise and click on the **Italic** button again to turn italics off.

6. **Step 3** - Select recipients.
    You may:
    - use an existing list;
      select from Outlook contacts;
      type a new list.

7. Select **Use an existing list**.

8. Select **Browse** and locate and click on the file containing your addresses and then click **Open**.

9. De-select from the list of people you do not wish to include in your mail merge.

10. Click **OK**.

11. **Step 4** - If you have not already done so write your letter now.

12. Add recipient information by clicking on the location in the document where you wish to add it and then click on the item you wish to add from the list in the **Task Pane** e.g. **Address Block**.

13. Click **Next** when you have finished writing your letter.

Mail Merge ▼ ✕
⊙ | ⊕ | ⌂
Select document type
What type of document are you working on?
⦿ Letters
○ E-mail messages
○ Envelopes
○ Labels
○ Directory
Letters
Send letters to a group of people. You can personalize the letter that each person receives.
Click Next to continue.
Step 1 of 6
⇨ Next: Starting document

14. **Step 5** - Preview your letters. This enables you to view what your final letters will look like.

15. **Step 6** - Once you are happy with your letters click on **Complete the merge**.

16. You can choose either to **Print** your letters or **Edit individual letters**.

✔ To open an existing presentation

1. Click on **File** and **Open**.

2. Click on the presentation you want to open and then click on **Open**.

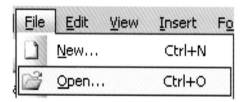

✔ To clear the screen

Click on **File** and then **Close**.

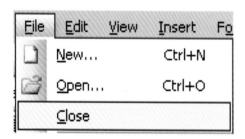

✔ To exit from PowerPoint

Click on **File** and then **Exit**.

✔ To create labels using Mail Merge

Using Mail Merge to create labels can be useful especially if you are sending out a large number of letters and do not wish to address each envelope yourself.

1. Start by creating and saving your **Data Source** (See above)

2. Click on **Tools, Letters and Mailings** and then **Mail Merge**.

3. Follow the instructions as written in the **Task Pane**. You may click forward and back once you have started this process.

4. **Step 1**- Select the type of document you are working on e.g. **Labels**.

5. **Step 2** - Select which document you wish to use e.g. **Start from existing document**.

6. Identify the type of label you are using (this should be printed on your box of labels) then select the **Label options** and select the label you are using. Click **OK**.

7. **Step 3** - Select the recipients. You may:
    use an existing list;
    select from Outlook contacts;
    type a new list.

8. Select **Use an existing list**.

9. Select **Browse** and locate and click on the file containing your addresses and then click **Open**.

10. **Step 4** - Arrange your labels by placing the address details in the order you wish them to appear on the label.

11. **Step 5** - Preview your labels. This enables you to view what your final labels will look like.

✔ Saving, opening and closing your presentation

Saving your presentations enables you to store and retrieve work that you have undertaken. This allows you to review, edit and re-use these presentations in the future.

✔ To save your presentation

1. Click on **File** and then **Save As**.

2. Click in the **File name** box and enter the name of your presentation e.g. **test**.

3. Click on the **Save** button.

✔ To save your presentation on a floppy disk

1. Click on **File** and then **Save As**.

2. Next to the **Save in** box click on the down arrow and choose **3½ Floppy**.

3. Click in the **File name** box and enter the name of your presentation e.g. **test**.

4. Click on the **Save** button.

12. **Step 6** - Once you are happy with your labels click on **Complete the merge**.

13. You can either choose to **Print** your labels or **Edit individual labels**.

✔ To create a whole sheet of identical labels

1. Click on **Tools, Letters and Mailings** and then **Envelopes and Labels**.

2. Click on the **Labels** tab and then **Options**.

3. Identify the type of label you are using (this should be printed on your box of labels) e.g.

   Label products: Avery A4 & A5 sizes
   Product number: L7160 – Address

4. Click on **OK**.

5. Within the **Address** box type in the address (or any other text you wish to appear on each label) e.g. **Kingston Primary School**.

6. Click on **New Document** to create your labels.

7. Place a sheet of labels in your printer and print.

✔ To print a single label

1. Complete steps 1 to 5 above.

2. Place a sheet of labels in your printer.

3. Under the heading **Print** select **Single label**.
   NB: This will print your label in the top left corner of your sheet unless you choose to change the **Row** and **Column** indicated.

4. Click on **Print**.

✔ To use the Task Pane

The **Task Pane** gives you a selection of options to make the creation of your presentation easier. Through the **Task Pane** you can:

> Create a New Presentation
> Open an existing presentation
> Use a Design Template

The **Task Pane** also relates to other features of PowerPoint and these will be discussed as they come up throughout this book.

✔ To use Slide Layout

Slide Layout enables you to select a template for each slide of your presentation. These allow you to add text, graphics, charts and graphs to your presentations. Alternatively, selecting a blank slide will enable you to place text boxes and graphics wherever you choose.

✔ To create a new presentation

1. Open PowerPoint.

2. Click on **Create a new presentation** (you will find this in the Task Pane on the right of your screen).

3. Click on **Blank Presentation**.

4. Click on the **Slide Layout** of your choice.

✔ To create macros

A macro is a series of commands and functions that can be run whenever you need to perform a specified task. Some macros can be extremely complex, but the instructions below guide you through the creation of a fairly simple macro.

1. Click on **Tools** and then **Macro**.

2. Click on **Record New Macro** and then give your macro a name e.g. **address**.

3. Under **Assign macro to** click on **Keyboard.**

4. Press the shortcut key you wish to use for your macro e.g. **Alt +A** (remember many shortcut keys are already assigned).

5. Click on **Assign** and then **Close**.

6. Perform the series of commands you wish to record e.g. type your address at the top of the page.

7. Click on the **Stop button** to stop recording your macro.

8. To run your macro press your shortcut key e.g. **Alt +A.**

client ✓

Contents

Word

 ## To use Word on a SMART Board

Using **Word** with a **SMART Board** allows you to work on documents with a group and save your annotations either in converted-to-text form or as freehand annotations.

 ## To save the annotation

1. With **Word** running, lift up a **Pen Tray Stylus**.

   The **Capture/Save toolbar** will appear.

2. Press the **Save Annotations** button.

   This will save the annotation in its current form inside a frame, which can then be moved and/or deleted as you wish.

 ## To save the annotation as text

1. With **Word** running, lift up a **Pen Tray Stylus**.

   The **Capture/Save toolbar** will appear.

2. Press the **Save Annotations as Text** button.

   This will convert the annotation to text and insert it at the cursor insertion point.

SMART
Technologies Inc.

40

Contents